PROFESSOR VALDOR AND THE GIANT LASER

Written by Jenny Feely

Illustrated by Alex Stitt

Flying Start
to Literacy®

Professor Valdor

Contents

Chapter 1
A new mission

Secret agents Roxby and Crispo had been called to a meeting with Inspector Morris at headquarters.

"We have a new mission for you," said the inspector. He pointed to a photo of the Arctic ice on his computer screen. Right in the middle, where there should have been thick white ice, there was a gaping hole with a red glow coming out of it.

"How did that hole get there?" asked Crispo. "That ice is more than 15 metres thick."

"We don't know. We sent a submarine under the ice to find out, but we lost contact. This is the last we heard from the USS Shadow," said Inspector Morris, pressing a button.

"Mayday, mayday. Our navigation systems have failed. May ..."

"Without navigation equipment, the USS Shadow will have to search for a break in the ice and return to the surface," said the inspector. "If they don't find a crack in the ice, they will run out of air."

Suddenly, there was a loud crackle from the inspector's computer. The evil, smirking face of Professor Valdor appeared on the screen.

"Ha ha!" screeched Valdor. "How do you like what I've done with my giant ice-melting laser?"

"Why should we care?" asked Crispo.

"Perhaps melting a little sea ice is not a big deal," said Valdor, "but what will happen when I melt all the ice in Greenland?"

Roxby turned pale. "The sea level would rise and most cities near the sea would be flooded!" she said. "What do you want, Valdor?"

"Well first, release my partner Dr Zardos from jail. Then, make me ruler of the world! Otherwise I will let my giant ice-melting laser loose on Greenland. And you can't stop me! My laser is so powerful that it will stop all navigation and communication equipment from working."

Suddenly, Valdor disappeared from the screen.

Chapter 2
The USS Armstrong

"Professor Valdor must be stopped," said Roxby, "before she causes a huge disaster."

"This will be your most difficult mission yet," said Inspector Morris, "but you must go to the Arctic, find Professor Valdor, and destroy her giant laser. The world is depending on you. But," he added, "I do have something that might help."

The inspector pushed a button and the wall slid back, revealing an underground dock and a shiny submarine. The crew all stood to attention.

"This is the USS Armstrong," said the secret agent scientist Dr Jackson. "This remote control activates the robotic arm and huge magnet. The magnet is powerful enough to pick up a submarine."

Crispo grabbed the remote control and started to fiddle with the buttons.

"Be careful!" yelled Dr Jackson, but it was too late – a white beam of light shot toward the water. In an instant the water had turned to ice.

"Wow!" said Crispo. "It's a freeze ray."

"And that's not all," said Dr Jackson. "Watch this!" The submarine suddenly vanished.

"Where did it go?" asked Crispo.

Hey!

CLICK!

SECRET AGENT

SECRET SC...TIS

SECR... SCIEN...

ZAP

"It's still there," said Dr Jackson. "We painted it with our new, top-secret paint. The paint can change colour. I just made it blue to blend in with the water." He pushed the button and the submarine reappeared.

"That's great," said Roxby. "But does it have navigation equipment that will still work if we are attacked by Professor Valdor's giant laser, so we can find our way under the ice?"

"I'm afraid not," said Dr Jackson. "That is why this will be your most difficult mission."

Chapter 3
Help from the past

Just then one of the crew stepped forward. It was an old sailor named Stan.

"Excuse me, sir," he said to the inspector, holding out an old, battered book. "I think I have an idea."

The inspector looked annoyed.

"What is it?" asked Roxby, before Inspector Morris could tell him to be quiet.

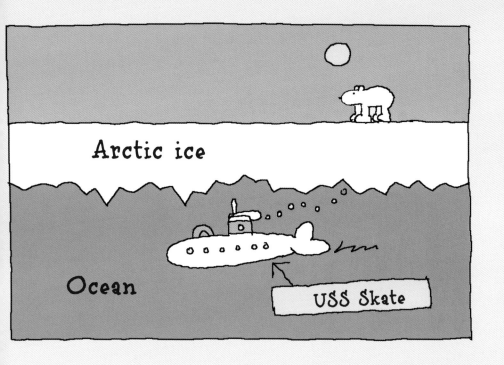

"Well," said Stan. "I was on the submarine USS Skate back in the 1950s. We were travelling under the Arctic ice and we had the same trouble. When we were deep below the ice, our navigation equipment stopped working and we got lost."

"Yes, yes," said the inspector impatiently. "That's a fascinating story, but we have important business to attend to."

"Wait," said Roxby, "let's hear what he has to say. What did you do?"

"Luckily we had an old journal made by Sir Hubert Wilkins. He was the first explorer to take a submarine under the Arctic ice, you know. He measured the depth of the ocean floor."

"How did that help you?" asked Crispo.

"We used those measurements to find out where we were. I took more measurements on other Arctic missions. The information in this notebook will help you find your way under the ice without navigation equipment," said the sailor.

"Fantastic," said Roxby. "You're coming with us." Roxby and Crispo leaped aboard the submarine.

"Good luck, secret agents Roxby and Crispo," said Inspector Morris. "You're our last hope."

Chapter 4
Under the ice

When Roxby and Crispo reached the Arctic ice, they couldn't believe their eyes.

"Wow, look at that," said Crispo. "The bottom of the ice isn't flat – it's all jagged. And just look at all those colours."

"It sure is beautiful under the ice," said Roxby. But no sooner had the words left her mouth than a loud alarm sounded.

Crispo looked at the control panel. "We've lost our navigation system," he said. "And our communication system has gone too."

"We must be close to Valdor's giant laser," said Roxby. "This ice all looks the same. I can see how USS Shadow got lost. Stan, take over the navigation!"

With Stan guiding the submarine, they steadily moved forward.

"We don't want Professor Valdor to know we are coming," said Roxby. "Let's make the submarine blue like the water."

With the flick of a button, the USS Armstrong seemed to disappear in the water. They travelled on and on until a strange red glow could be seen coming out of a huge dome-like submarine that rested on the bottom of the ocean.

"It's Valdor's headquarters," said Roxby. "Activate the freeze ray."

Crispo aimed the ray at the top of the dome. A beam of white light shot out toward it, freezing all the water in its path. As the freeze ray hit the red light coming out of Valdor's submarine, it caused a great cloud of steam. The freeze ray and the giant laser were battling each other.

At first, the freeze ray was stronger. But slowly and surely, the giant laser got stronger and stronger. Then it began to move – back along the ice trail in the water, toward the USS Armstrong.

"Oh, no! Professor Valdor has figured out where we are by following the ice in the water!" yelled Roxby.

"The laser's heat ray is aimed right at us!" yelled Crispo. "We're heating up." He looked at the temperature gauge. It was rising quickly.

"We have to stop that heat ray," said Roxby. "If our submarine gets much hotter, it will melt!"

"But how can we stop it?" asked Crispo.

Chapter 5
Changing colour

"What colour can we make this submarine?" asked Roxby.

"Any of the colours on this panel," said Crispo.

Roxby quickly looked at the panel. "Try white," she said. Crispo used the controls to select white.

"It's still getting hotter," said Crispo.

"Try red," said Roxby. Crispo changed the controls.

"It's not working," said Crispo. "I can hardly touch the computer, it's so hot."

"Try that shiny colour!" said Roxby.

Crispo changed the controls again. Suddenly, the submarine turned bright and shiny – just like a mirror.

Roxby and Crispo held their breath and waited. The submarine started to cool.

"It's working! It's working!" shouted Crispo. "The mirror-like surface of the submarine is reflecting the heat away from us."

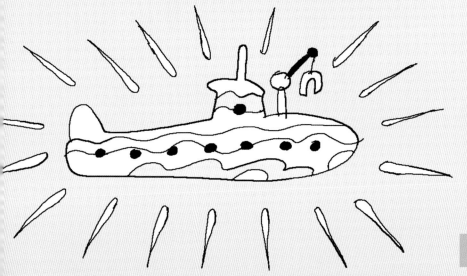

Then Roxby and Crispo noticed something amazing. The laser's heat ray was bouncing back from their submarine – onto itself! The dome-like submarine at the bottom of the sea was beginning to glow even brighter and starting to bulge.

"It's going to explode!" said Crispo.

At the last moment, a small escape pod shot out of the side of the submarine. Then – KABOOM! Professor Valdor's submarine and her giant laser exploded into millions of pieces.

"Quick," called Roxby, watching the escape pod. "Valdor's getting away."

Crispo aimed the freeze ray at the pod and fired. Without the giant laser to protect her, Valdor's escape pod was soon trapped in so much ice that it couldn't move. Crispo activated the submarine's magnetic arm.

"Got you!" he said, as the pod stuck fast.

Without delay, Roxby pointed the freeze ray at the hole in the ice. Slowly but surely, the hole closed over.

Chapter 6
Mission complete

With the giant laser destroyed, the submarine's navigation and communication systems were soon back to normal.

"USS Shadow, come in USS Shadow," Crispo called over the radio.

"This is USS Shadow," came a voice through the radio. "Everyone is okay and our communication and navigation systems are working again. We will see you back at headquarters. Over and out!"

"Calling USS Armstrong, attention USS Armstrong!" came Inspector Morris's voice over the radio.

"USS Armstrong receiving loud and clear," said Roxby. "We're happy to report that we have captured Professor Valdor and destroyed her giant laser."

"Well done, Roxby and Crispo," said the inspector. "You have saved the world again!"

A note from the author

I love secret agent stories and thought it would be fun to connect the story of the first voyage under the Arctic ice, which I wrote about in the book *Under the Ice*, with a fantastic mission for secret agents Roxby and Crispo.

I also based this story on a real event. In 1958, the navy submarine USS Skate had problems with its navigation equipment while under the Arctic ice and the crew used measurements made by Sir Hubert Wilkins to find their way to safety.

As this is a fantasy story, I had fun making up amazing secret devices such as the colour-changing paint on the submarine.